Praise
Relics of the Heart: St

"Having read these simple and well-t[...] real life experiences, he focuses on the life that most of the population has. Activities as simple as getting together to eat, celebrating a birth or going on vacation are very important moments for daily happiness, in the existence of this long road we call a fulfilled year, on which we are cementing the concept of family. The family is not only a group of people; it is something more important. The family is the basis of society, in which we should be grateful to our grandparents, to our parents, for the principles and values with which they raised us and we should act with the obligation to transmit them to future generations. This is what this book teaches us and reminds us that we should always be better people.."

— Manuel Gómez

"*Relics of the Heart* is a must-read for these times when time is scarce. So, then? Well, we must make space for its necessary reading. A space that will not take much time, since *Relics of the Heart* is so delicious that it is devoured and, at the same time, lingering on the palate after reading it. Racing against the clock of life, Oscar Fuentes has hurried to collect anecdotes of his father, stories and memories before the old man leaves, and with him, his story. And so, we are faced with a family album, one of those that keep the photos of our celebrations, great events and happy moments. *Relics of the Heart* is that album, an archive of his family as only the poet of Miami's Biscayne Bay, The Biscayne Poet, can achieve. A trip to the past, to a sunny afternoon at the grandparents' house in the San Cristobal neighborhood of Honduras. A cockfight in Siguatepeque. The smell of chicken soup with coconut milk. A ship full of Honduran coffee. And Manhattan. His Manhattan, birthplace of the author. Fuentes tells us all about it. The tears and the sweat. The laughter and the happiness. The ups and downs. All the results of living. *Relics of the Heart* is a Latin-American and at the same time, universal, story. We identify with it. The author has given us a great gift with this book. This is a gift that comes from the heart. With it, he invites us to remember our roots and reflect on them because time is short. Because, as the author has well known, to know how we got to where we are and why we are the way we are, we have to go back to who and where we came from."

— Miguel Garrote

"With *Relics of the Heart*, Oscar transports us back in time with delicacy, letting us feel the legacy of his family's stories with poetic nostalgia. Pages that describe a world of dense memories of life, give value to the union of family affections that he narrates with grace and detail."

— Claudio Marcotulli

"Oscar takes us to the sweet and luminous land of childhood, to the warmth of home, to unconditional love. We travel with him as spectators of the anecdotes of a family united by love, their encounters and misunderstandings, from his grandparents to his parents, uncles, aunts, cousins and brothers. The strength and love of the women in his family are clearly delineated and weave that family union that is the engine to move forward despite the difficulties and complexities of life. In Grandma Fina I found traces of my own grandmother and nostalgically returned to her warm lap where I always felt safe. These little stories have that virtue of bringing us back to the happy moments of our lives. The stories are not foreign to the cultural environment and "Cockfighting" stands out among them, a tradition that touches all of us Latin Americans and that is as picturesque as it is real."

— Claudia Solis

Cover Design Copyright © 2024 by Nila Duranza
Edited by Flor Ana Mireles

1st Edition | 01
Paperback ISBN: 979-8-9895551-8-5

First Published July 2024

For inquiries and bulk orders, please email:
indieearthbooks@gmail.com

Printed in the United States of America   1 2 3 4 5 6 7 8 9

Indie Earth Publishing Inc.
| Miami, FL |

www.indieearthbooks.com

INDIE EARTH
PUBLISHING

Relics of the Heart:

Stories of My Family

Oscar Fuentes
alias
The Biscayne Poet

Acknowledgments

First and foremost, I offer my deepest gratitude to my aunts, uncles, and cousins from both sides of my family, who generously shared their stories with me, helping to piece together scattered bits of our history like a puzzle until the full picture emerged. Thank you to my beautiful wife, Carmen, for her unwavering support in all my artistic and multidisciplinary projects; her selfless encouragement keeps a part of my heart wild and untamed.

I am immensely grateful to my mother and father for the sacrifices they made throughout their life journey so that my sister, brother, and I could have a better future. Their selfless, unconditional love has been a profound source of inspiration, guiding me to be a loving son, husband, and the best father I can be for my children. While no family is perfect, I have learned that recognizing our imperfections helps us comprehend, forgive, and accept ourselves and our loved ones, and to take responsibility for how we live our lives and tell our family story.

I also extend my heartfelt thanks to my publisher, Indie Earth, and editor, Flor Ana, who encouraged me to pursue this book to honor my father's principles and humility, to preserve his memory, and to live my life appreciating the values my ancestors cherished.

A special thank you goes to my sister Gissel, Toño, Marcos, Emily, Victoria, Camila, Katia, Andres, Daniel, Valeria, Belkis, Milagros, Ricardo, Chad, Sophy, Marcelo, Natacha, Mariana, and Maria for all the love they bring to our beautiful family today. I want to thank my uncles Alonso and Marcos, who were always very loving and special to me when I was a young child, curious about their trumpet playing and their soccer skills on the field. They will always be remembered with so much love and admiration.

Lastly, my gratitude extends to you, my readers. I know we share similarities in our lives, as we are all united in unraveling the knots of our histories and celebrating our journeys, no matter the distances lived or yet to discover within.

Relics of the Heart:

Stories of My Family

Oscar Fuentes

For my parents and my family

Introduction
José Ramón Alonso-Lorea

Oscar Fuentes has ignited my soul, that perpetual immateriality that acquires vigor within a family fabric. He has touched the heartstrings of those of us who are children, by a natural logic, and parents, for an illuminated chosen reason. He has shared with me, with the utmost modesty and intellectual honesty, his latest book project which he dedicates to his father, "who faces the challenge of Alzheimer's in its most severe form." Entitled *Relics of the Heart*, this collection of short stories recounts the origins of her family and includes "stories my father used to tell me. It is, in essence, a project in honor of his memory." Oscar assures me that "I dream of being able to read these stories in person to my father, as well as to my grandfather, who will be 99 years old in January 2025." A beautiful idea.

I don't know if Oscar is aware that his project provides an answer to two questions of cultural creation in the last two hundred years: what can be done to bring art and literature closer to real life? How to transform people's lives through art and literature? Oscar's book has the answers and, in doing so, brings us back to the cycle of the true value of culture: to heal. Alzheimer's is a dementia that causes problems with memory and ends up limiting people's quality of life. One of the fundamental therapies to face this deterioration is the use of cognitive stimulation. Oscar's book, read or consulted with his father repeatedly, is an effective tool for memory training, even for psychosocial activation and physical exercise, as the story can be dramatized. Oscar himself assures us in his presentation that his father "could always tell stories full of acted narration." In fact, that these oral stories, "with a dramatic tension and climax, provoked screams and agile movements of action with scars marked on his body." Those scars, associated with the stories in the book, are marks that contain the emotional aspects that trigger the events of the past. They are his father's way of mapping the memory. They are mnemonic resources that aid memory. Let us not forget that with similar techniques traditional family societies, and those that developed in pre-writing times, preserved their millenary traditions.

As I understand it, Oscar's book also confronts another type of "political Alzheimer's," fictitious and dangerous. In these "pandemic" times of organized attempts, of the dissolution of families through bio-politics and birth control, of the dissolution of traditions and even of nations, Oscar's book becomes irreverent, anti-globalizing and patriotic. And when I refer to this last term, I focus my attention on that small and intimate, filial and consanguineous homeland, which is the smallest and most powerful social cell born with the sapiens: the family structure. There was a time, in the times of Ortega & Gasset, when there was talk of the "dehumanization" of art. Today, even more regrettably, there is an attempt to dehumanize, to tear apart, to denaturalize, the large family cell that is the triumphant protagonist in Oscar's stories.

There are no pretensions in this book by Oscar Fuentes to seek an avant-garde literature or a renewal of isms. There is no interest in narrative experimentation or neologisms, nor in hermetic and unreadable writing. No, none of that matters here. In this book, there is a natural humanism in the description of the environments, a calm effort to reconstruct and order a familiar past with a healing intention. Yet, the story and the way it is told are emotional, not because of a therapeutic yearning. The book finally stimulates the desire to imitate the narrator, to remake through writing our own family stories.

In these family stories, there is transparency and honesty as literary resources, if they can be called as such. It is a simple and plain description of the filial. What is filial, if not the relationship between sons and fathers (mothers and daughters are already included in the generic)? The author presents us with four toasts (with rum, beer, coffee and wine, respectively) that are libations to the interior of the body, which seek to externalize memories protected in deep areas of the memory and allow us to introduce the characters. Children who toast and introduce their parents. Grandchildren to their grandparents. Brothers to brothers. Aunts to the nephew-author of this book. The description of the birth of Gissel, Armando's firstborn, the narrator's sister, the one who was born to live in the "heart of those present" is striking; it has a dramatic and emotional force that those of us who are parents feel deeply. In order to write outstanding family moments, the narrator weaves a web that projects from different nodes of memory. For example: a stone, the cab driver and an aunt Miriam of great courage; the special and heroic uncle Gerardo and Spielberg's *ET*; father Oscar, the bicycle, the road and the sugarcane field; the farewell to grandmother Fina, the departure for Miami and the memory of Vicks VapoRub. That omnipresent grandmother who rises from the narrator's psyche. "Nostalgia" and "tradition." How many of us long for those Sunday lunches with Grandma? That chicken soup with coconut milk seasoned with love. Oscar's family memories strike a chord with this reader. I can appreciate the weight of enduring moral values, the "endless possibilities" of the guava tree in the backyard, and even smell the enticing aroma of that Honduran coffee at Grandma Fina's house.

Contents

Contents

Relics of the Heart:

Stories of My Family

Oscar Fuentes

Relics of the Heart

"I come from a family of storytellers. My father, for example, could always tell stories filled with an acted narrative that fed mine and my siblings' imaginations. Stories with dramatic tension and climaxes that provoked screams and agile movements of action, with scars marked on his body as evidence to the fantastic events that only he could have told.

The following collection of stories is my homage to my father and his tales, which to this day, I don't know if they were invented at the time or if they were detailed and memorized. In this dedication to him, I also try to combat his Alzheimer's disease, for through him, I choose to remember many of the narrative details that were part of the events that had to occur for me to be able to be here telling you this—things and details with a minimal dose of fiction, images that I chose to remember and that at the same time put me in front of many other things that I also hope someday to forget.

Naturally, as you can see, Alzheimer's takes away the luxury of choosing which things to forget and which things to remember, transforming our memories of all that we have lived and suffered into loose leaves drifting in the wind, like petals that float eternally.

In this struggle against forgetting, I tried to tell the origin stories of my parents, my grandparents and also those memories that marked my childhood and that were part of my training, like lessons of emotional and family education.

I hope that these stories also serve as an opportunity to be interested with some curiosity in the adventures and sacrifices of our families, people who raised us with much love and hope. It is our turn today to be able to tell and remember, as an act or gesture of gratitude and love, preserving these stories as *Relics of the Heart*."

Oscar Armando Fuentes Jr.

This picture captures my grandparents, Fina and Carlos, during their one and only trip to Miami in the mid-90s. Back then, we lived in a cute little blue house off 32nd Ave and 19th Terrace. I remember arriving in my car from Coral Gables High and seeing my grandmother, who had just arrived from Honduras, out in the front yard with tears of joy in her eyes. It had been about 10 years since I had last seen them. They looked beautiful and happy, just as I had always remembered them, but I was no longer the 8-year-old boy they had said goodbye to one distant Honduran afternoon.

Grandparents Zuniga

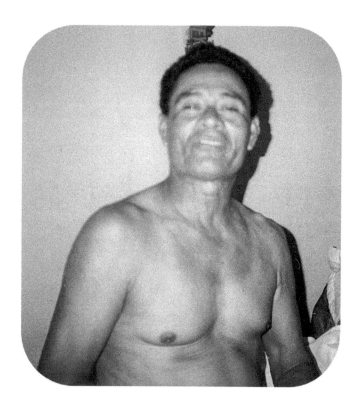

I remember my grandfather's hard hands. I remember his smile every day when he came home from work, and I would jump off that guava tree and run to hug him hello.

Oak and Tenderness

Scene:
Outside of the grandparents' house, it is a sunny afternoon in Carpules. You can see a table with several chairs, where Gerardo, Alonso and Armandito are sitting, enjoying a few drinks of rum. Soft and nostalgic music can be heard in the background.

Gerardo: [Raises his glass] *Cheers, family! To our parents, Carlos and Fina, who taught us the true meaning of love and dedication.*

Alonso: [Nods his head] *Cheers! They really were role models. I remember how Papi Carlos always told us stories about his life in Aguas Calientes, and Mami Fina, with her sweetness, gave us advice that still resonated in our hearts.*

Armandito: [Smiling] *Yes, it is incredible how her love and commitment have marked us all. And to think that it all started in elementary school. Can you imagine that today?*

Gerardo: [Laughing] *Not in my wildest dreams! But that was their story, as authentic and beautiful as they were. And look how their family grew, eight children who became professionals and good people.*

Alonso: [Reflecting] *And let's not forget the sacrifice they made for Juan Carlos, Miriam's son. Raising him as their own son and supporting him and seeing him become a doctor was a real triumph for them and now he is even a father of a family.*

Armandito: [Nodding with emotion] *Yes, it was an immense act of love. It is incredible how the Zuniga family unites in difficult times and finds the strength to move forward.*

Gerardo: [Raising his glass again] *So, today we toast to our parents, to their legacy of love, sacrifice and united family. I know my little sister is in* *heaven feeling very proud of her son. Cheers!*

Alonso y Armandito: *Cheers!*

[The three of them clink their glasses in a gesture of camaraderie while the sun begins to set on the horizon, illuminating the sky with warm and golden tones.]

I chose this picture because my sister looks so sweet in her innocence. That's me standing on a bench next to her. It's not my most complimentary photo, but this image captures us on a stage with red curtains, something that, through the years, we would both become very familiar with in the artistic upbringing our parents were able to provide.

I borrowed this photo from my sister's family photo album. I absolutely love this photograph of my uncles Gerardo and Alonso and my grandparents Fina and Carlos. They are celebrating one of my grandmother's birthdays, or is it their wedding anniversary? I get emotionally happy when I see their radiant smiles. Our entire Zuniga family smiles this happily, by the way.

Carlos and Fina

My grandparents, Carlos Zuniga Reyes and María Josefina Juárez, met in elementary school. My mom tells me that my grandparents fell in love when they were very young, and that, when they finished elementary school, they were already living together in Aguas Calientes, in the majestic mountain of Merendón.

Eventually, they married, and so Maria Josefina Juarez and Carlos Zuniga Reyes had eight children: Gloria, Alonzo, Yamile, Miriam, Gerardo, Lupe, Julia and Eldy. My mother, Gloria Esperanza, the eldest, trained as a nursing assistant. My uncle Carlos Alonso gained a Bachelor's degree in Economics, my aunts Maria Yamile and Rosa Lidia (or Miriam) studied secretarial work while my uncle Gerardo specialized in cabinetmaking and fine carpentry. My Aunt Guadalupe worked as a social worker and then as a teacher, and my aunts Julia Isabel and Eldy Janet obtained degrees in Public Accounting.

My mother tells me that my aunt Miriam was discovered by a beauty modeling agent and was invited to participate in the "Mis Choloma" beauty pageant. On the day of the beauty pageant, my aunt won second place in the competition, but at home, her whole family crowned her as the winner and surrounded her with that unconditional Zuniga love.

My grandfather Carlos, shortly before his twentieth birthday, had the opportunity to work for the Tela Railroad Company, where he remained for more than thirty years in the agricultural department of the company. Agriculture came naturally to him as he had grown up in his homeland of Aguas Calientes working in livestock and agriculture. He was a man of the land, and if he were to be compared to a tree, it would be an oak. Strong and industrious men like him are rare to find in this world.

I remember some afternoons when he would return to Grandma Fina's house with unusual animals, from giant snakes in a sack to huge black iguanas and even armadillos. In Calpules lived a man by the name of Quinn, who had an animal export business and would buy any rare or exotic creature that people brought to him. From time to time, my grandfather would sell these animals that he found while working in the fields of the Tela Railroad Company.

Despite the modest salary from his work at the Tela, my grandfather Carlos and my grandmother Fina supported and loved each other with tenderness and respect. This exemplary relationship allowed them to instill in their eight children the importance of education and the necessary preparation for life. The story of my grandparents is unique, but at the same time universal, because in them, my siblings and I also found our happiness during our childhood. Today I understand that their family love is a testimony to the value that is taught more by example than by words.

Perhaps my grandparents' most powerful gesture of love and parental guidance was raising my cousin Juan Carlos, son of my aunt Miriam. When Juan Carlos was just a child, my aunt had to make the difficult decision to migrate to Miami in search of a better salary in order to provide a more stable future for her son. Over the years, my aunt was diagnosed with advanced cancer and her health deteriorated rapidly.

I remember clearly the day my aunt passed away. I was the only one of the Zuniga family present at the hospital. By a strange coincidence of life, in those same days Doña Maria, the mother of Manolo Gomez, my aunt Lupe's mother-in-law, also passed away, and while I was being informed of my aunt Miriam's departure, Manolo, Lupe and Yamile were at Manolo's mother's wake. I cried all that night for my aunt and for all the sadness that had overwhelmed us in those days.

I was told that her funeral was attended by many people. My grandparents, Carlos and Fina, raised Juan Carlos with so much love and parental guidance that the young man became an exemplary medical student in college. He graduated with a doctor's degree, and throughout all those years, my grandparents were by his side, filled with pride in their grandson who was a doctor, as if it were a promise fulfilled to their daughter Miriam, a promise that symbolized the work of parents and grandparents that was passed down through generations.

Grandpa Toño

Circa 1990s. There was something about my grandfather Tono that demanded your attention when he walked by or entered the room. My father's father had charm and an assertive attitude when he spoke. He had a collection of hats and wore one every day in his youth. I know for sure my hat fixation comes from him. He was a complex yet simple man, always with a plan in mind or a carpentry project in the works. Skilled with his hands and good with his words. I feel that I carry my grandfather's essence simply by being a member of his family and carrying his last name.

A Man For History

Scene:
First floor of the grandparents' house in Colonia San Cristóbal, a sunny afternoon. Cousins Junior, Enock, Gissel, Carlos and Oscarito are sitting around a table, enjoying some cold beers. Soft, relaxing music plays in the background

Junior: [Raises his beer bottle] *Cheers, cousins! To our grandparents, Antonio and Nena, who taught us the true meaning of family and resilience.*

Gissel: [Nods her head] *Cheers! Without a doubt, their story is an example of overcoming and unconditional love.*

Enock: [Smiling] *I remember the stories mom used to tell us about how Grandpa Antonio was respected as any great doctor in La Lima; he was the macho man, the man with the key to the whole alley!*

Carlos: [Nodding] *Yes, and let's not forget that he was the manager of the bowling alley in La Lima Nueva. He worked hard there to support his family.*

Oscarito: [Looking around the house in admiration] *Grandpa Toño was the master of his house, of the San Cristobal neighborhood and of the sun. His presence was like a lighthouse that illuminated everything around him.*

Junior: [Remembering] *And how he taught us all to be strong and to fight for what we wanted! That determination and leadership is part of his legacy - something he also instilled in our parents.*

Enock: [Reflecting] *Yes, they definitely left an indelible mark on our lives. We will always remember them with love and gratitude.*

Gissel: [Raising her bottle] *So, today we toast to our grandparents Toño* *and Nena, for being examples of strength, courage, love and wisdom. Cheers!*

Carlos, Oscarito, Junior y Enock: *Cheers!*

[The cousins clink their bottles in a gesture of camaraderie, while the sun slowly sets on the Honduran horizon, bathing the house in a warm golden light.]

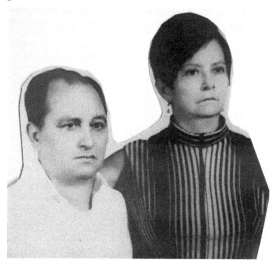

1972. This picture of my grandmother Nena carrying two babies is so special. On one arm, she has my sister Gissel, and on her other arm, my cousin Enock. It makes me think of the passage of time and how looking at this photo is almost like traveling back to a time when my grandmother celebrated her first grandchildren in a growing Fuentes family of more grandbabies to come, who would eventually try their best to change the world for the better.

Toño and Nena

The moving story of my grandfather, Antonio Vinicius Fuentes, takes us to the charming corner of Punta Caliente, Honduras, in 1920. However, his arrival in the world was marked by deep melancholy, as he lost his mother when he was only nine years old. That early loss left an indelible mark on his heart, and his mother's shadow became his constant companion ever since, like an echo from the past.

After his mother's departure, Antonio found refuge in the warm arms of a close friend of hers, who became his protector and cared for him with love until youth knocked on his door.

Eventually, when youth came along, Antonio decided to strike out on his own and moved to the city of La Lima. There he found employment with the Tela Railroad Company, a railroad company that would be his second home for more than twenty-five years. Under that working roof, Antonio carved his destiny, acquiring skills and knowledge that would accompany him throughout his life.

But fate had surprises in store. During his time in the city, Antonio crossed paths with a woman who would change his life forever: María Zulema, affectionately known as my grandmother Nena. They fell deeply in love and decided to unite their lives in marriage, moving into a humble house in a neighborhood called Punta Caliente, giving birth to a family that would grow and flourish over time. Together, they became the proud parents of eight children: Marcos, Reynaldo, Clarita, Oscar, Rosita, Zulema, Salvador and Patricia.

Through tireless effort and boundless dedication, Antonio was able to provide for his extended family. His constant work and fighting spirit were the pillars that sustained the family, like characters in an endearing real-life novel, where tenacity and love were poignantly intertwined.

But one gloomy day, while Maria Zulema was in the Punta Caliente house with her first three children, an unexpected disaster shook their lives. The fire, which started two wooden houses on the same block, engulfed everything and the speed of the blaze did not give them enough time to save most of their belongings from the fire.

When my grandfather, Antonio, arrived home to find the devastation, everyone was there, watching helplessly as their home went up in flames, tears in their eyes. Antonio embraced everyone with love and relief that they were unharmed. The house was gone, and so were most of their possessions.

In the months that followed, the family took refuge in the home of a neighboring friend, while my grandfather, with the support and generous donations of all those who worked with him at the Tela Railroad Company, acquired a half-hectare plot of land in San Cristobal. It was there that he built the two-story house that would become the family's new home.

This house stood as a living testimony to the effort, unity and solidarity of the family and the surrounding community. Each brick laid was an act of love and determination, as if they were writing a new chapter in their moving story of overcoming.

In this photo, we are in the backyard of my grandfather's house in San Cristobal, sitting on the edge of a plunge pool he had built many years before when my dad was a young man. The photo was taken in 1998. I was visiting from Miami after Hurricane Mitch hit Honduras in late October that year. It was one of the deadliest Atlantic hurricanes, causing extensive damage and loss of life in the region. So, at this time in this photo, it is when I took my first pause from school to go check on my family. The second and final pause from school would come a few years later when I became a dad and had to work full-time to be the responsible man I was born to be.

In 2021, my parents celebrated their 50th wedding anniversary. My friend Alexandra stopped by to take pictures of all of us to commemorate the occasion. In this beautiful photo, I can feel their entire journey and understand their love and happiness.

My Parents

1971, Tegucigalpa, Honduras. That's the year my parents got married. Right after their wedding, my grandmother Nena, as a wedding gift, rented their honeymoon house in Tegucigalpa, where they spent time away from home in San Pedro Sula, honeymooning and planning and dreaming about all the possibilities in their new life together as husband and wife.

True Love

Escena:
Inside a cozy coffee shop, where Clarita, Gloria and Aide are seated at a table, enjoying their drinks while chatting animatedly

Clarita: [Raises her coffee cup] *How nice it is to be here together, girls! It's been a long time since we've had a date like this.*

Gloria: [Nods with a smile] *Yes, it's wonderful to be able to share this time together, remembering old times and creating new memories.*

Aide: [Settling into her chair] *Definitely. Besides, today is a special day for Gloria, isn't it, sister?*

Gloria: [With an illuminated look] *Yes! Today is 53 years since I met Armando.*

Clarita: [Intrigued] *Tell us more about that, sister-in-law! I've always been fascinated by how you met.*

Gloria: [Smiling] *Well, you know that Armando and I are from different worlds. He worked in construction and I was a nurse. But it all started at a bus stop near the Leonardo Martínez Valenzuela Hospital....*

[She dives into the story of how they met, describing how Armando approached her with nervousness but determination, and how an instant connection between them emerged.]

Aide: [Impressed] *What a beautiful story! It sounds like a scene out of a romantic movie.*

Clarita: [Excited] *And to think that that meeting marked the beginning of such an incredible love story, I remember that Armandon, my husband, had to go to see Don Carlos to ask for his hand, since my* *dad couldn't go because of work. How was the wedding afterwards?*

Gloria: [With nostalgia] *The wedding was an unforgettable day. We celebrated at El Barracón, with the whole family together. My father, always so proud, even built a makeshift bar for the occasion.*

[They continue to share details of the wedding and the happy memories they have shared over the years.]

Clarita: [Raising her cup] *To true love and memories that last forever. Cheers!*

Gloria y Aide: *Cheers!*

[They toast with their cups, enjoying the moment and the company while the aroma of coffee and the murmur of the cafeteria envelop them.]

1971, Tegucigalpa, Honduras. That's the year my parents got married. My dad was 18 years of age, and my mom was 20. In this photo, they stand outside their rented honeymoon house, embracing a love that has stayed with them until today. A union of love that, in so many ways, has been the catalyst to a love that influences the same kind of love my siblings and I give to our individual families today.

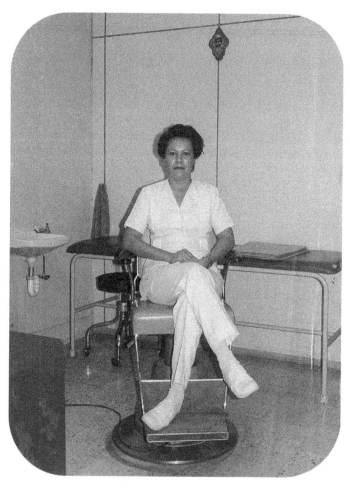

Circa late 1970s. I remember the times when my mom used to take me to her job at the hospital. I don't remember much of her actual job there; the only thing I remember clearly was the lunch hour. We used to walk over to a little cafeteria right outside the hospital where I found the food to be memorably delicious. I used to love unzipping and opening her purse and breathing in the minty scent of the chewing gum package in there. She used to wear a small white hat that was part of her white uniform, and I used to fall in love with my mom every time I saw her dressed for work.

Oscar Armando Fuentes Aguirre
& Gloria Esperanza Zuniga

My father relates that when he was 17, my grandfather took him to enroll at the Air Force base near San Pedro Sula's international airport, which was a short distance from his home in San Cristobal. He had been getting into too many fights, and Grandpa Toño feared that something bad would happen to him if he didn't straighten up his life at an early age.

The Air Force seemed like the perfect solution. My father recalls that when they arrived at the admissions office, they were told that all the slots were filled and that they would have to wait until next year, when recruiting sessions would begin again. On his way back home, my grandfather made it clear to my father that he needed to do something positive with his life so that he would not end up living on the streets, that he needed to straighten his path; otherwise, he would have to look for a job to help with expenses at home.

The next day, my father saw an ad in the newspaper looking for cooks to work aboard a cargo ship traveling to Europe. Those interested had to be willing to commit to a 12-month contract.

According to my father, my grandfather was very supportive of this job opportunity, even though my father was only 17 years old. Eight months passed, and his job on the ship had a work schedule of 40 hours a week, with time off for recreation and rest. The cargo ship carried hundreds of containers filled to the brim with Honduran coffee, roasted or decaffeinated, the country's main export, accounting for 22% of Honduras' total export earnings. The ship had already made stops in the eight countries scheduled on its shipping route, including the Netherlands, Germany, Belgium, France, the United Kingdom, Italy, Spain and Portugal.

Its last stop was Monrovia, Liberia, a common stopover for ships due to its strategic location in West Africa. My father tells a story of a trip back to Honduras, when one of the older sailors, who for no reason at all, did not like my father from the first day he boarded the ship. This older sailor liked to get drunk on his days off, and on a foggy night, when my father was leaning on the edge of the stern of the ship, watching the sharks eat the ship's debris, this sailor appeared out of nowhere, grabbed him from behind in a choke hold, laughing. In those days, it was not uncommon for a man to fall overboard and disappear into the water, and my father feared for his life. He tells how he had to find the strength he didn't have to free himself from the sailor's stranglehold, stomped his toes hard with his right leg, hit him in the stomach with his elbow, turned to face him and hit him in the face with his right hand, and the man recoiled. That's when the sailor grabbed a 2x4 plank of wood, and my father lunged across the floor toward a hammer that had been left there with other tools. The sailor swung the plank of wood toward my father's head, and my father swung the hammer at the plank, splitting it in two.

The sailor then lunged at my father in a blind, drunken rage, intent on pushing him over the edge, my father threw the hammer with his right arm and hit the sailor in the center of the forehead, knocking him down.

"You killed him!" someone shouted in the distance, running towards them through the fog of the night.

"What have you done, young man? You killed him, look at all that blood!" the man continued nervously.

"He's not dead, look at him, he's breathing, he's also very drunk, and besides, he attacked me, he tried to throw me overboard," my father said nervously and agitated.

Three more sailors arrived and took the sailor away. The ship's captain appeared through the fog, smoking a cigar, walking, limping toward my father.

"Are you all right, boy?"

"Yes, Captain, he attacked me from behind and wanted to throw me overboard, and I..."

The captain interrupted him with:

"Yes, I know, boy, I saw the whole thing from the upper deck, but this wooden leg didn't allow me to get there in time to stop the fight."

"So, I'm not in trouble?" my father asked.

"No, you're not in trouble because you didn't kill him with that hammer. Get out of here and go rest."

"Thank you, captain!" said my father, walking away, feeling relieved.

Back at the Port of Cortes, Honduras, my father waited with his bag of clothes over his shoulder, while my grandfather exchanged a few last words with the captain, shaking hands and walking away from the ship in my father's direction.

On the trip back to San Cristobal, they didn't say a word to each other, my father was sure he was in deep trouble with his dad, but just as they entered the San Cristobal colony, my grandfather said to him:

"Yesterday your friend Chico came by looking for you, he said that you should get in touch with him, that he got you a job as a masonry helper." It was then, in 1971, that he met my mother, Gloria Esperanza Zúñiga, at a bus stop near the Leonardo Martínez Valenzuela Hospital.

"It was 2:00 pm, and my father and his friend Chico were laying cement blocks across the street from the Leonardo Martinez Valenzuela Hospital in San Pedro Sula. They were adding an extra room to a small single-family house, and both sat on plastic buckets upside down on scaffolding 16 feet high. They worked together in a rhythm: cement, block, tap with the wooden handle of the masonry tool, level and repeat.

"At 2:30 p.m., the alarm on Chico's watch began to ring. My father finished the last piece of cement on the last block, while Chico poured hot black coffee into two small cups and handed one to my father.

"Then, they heard the hospital bell ring.

:They sat there drinking their coffee and waiting for all the beautiful hospital nurses to leave the building. They had been admiring the nurses in their white uniforms for almost a month, and my father had his eye on one nurse in particular.

"He had heard the other nurses call her by name and learned that her name was Gloria, but he wanted to know more about her, dreamed of meeting her someday, falling in love with her and even marrying her.

"Suddenly, the front doors of the hospital opened and the crowd of nurses dressed in white, with their white caps and white shoes, came out in all directions.

Oscar: [Looking at Gloria with determination] *Chico, today is the day. I can't just dream anymore. Gloria is my birthday present to myself.*

Chico: [Smiling] *Go ahead, Oscar! Go and talk to her.*

[Oscar combs and curls his hair, climbs down from the construction scaffolding and approaches Gloria (my mom) while she waits at the bus stop.]

Oscar: [Nervous, but determined] *Hi! My name is Oscar Armando Fuentes. Sorry if this sounds a little strange, but today is my birthday, and I've been looking forward to meeting you for a long time.*

Gloria: [Surprised and smiling] *Happy birthday, Oscar Armando Fuentes! I am Gloria Esperanza Zúñiga. Did you really intend to meet me?*

Oscar: [Smiling with relief] *Yes, Gloria. I've been watching you for the past few weeks and somehow today I felt I had to take the plunge and say "hello."*

Gloria: [Flattered] *That's very sweet, Oscar. I had noticed you too.*

[Oscar and Gloria begin to talk animatedly as they wait for the bus together. They discover common interests and feel a special connection.]

[Finally, Gloria's bus arrives.]

Gloria: [Preparing to board] *I have to get on the bus, Oscar. It's time to go back to my neighborhood, Calpules.*

Oscar: [Walking her to the bus] *I understand, Gloria. It's been a pleasure meeting you.*

[They say goodbye with a smile, and my mom gets on the bus. My dad watches her walk away and then heads back to the construction scaffolding where Chico is waiting for him.]

Chico: [Anxious] *Oscar! How did it go?*

[My father returns to work with a smile on his face, hoping that this is the start of something special.]

Oscar: [With a dream in his eyes] *Unbelievable. Her name is Gloria Esperanza. Gloria Esperanza, Gloria Esperanza, Gloria Esperanza.*

My dad tells how three months later, they got married in the Catholic church in Ciudad La Lima, that my grandfather Toño had rented a big bus to bring my mom's whole family from Calpules to the church and that someone had written on the outside, "Just Married," and then they tied a bunch of empty cans with string to the back of the bus so they would make noise against the pavement as they drove, and that they said their vows with the Virgin of Suyapa watching them, and that it was the best party in the history of Calpules.

My mom tells that the wedding party took place at El Barracón, that my grandmother Fina and her sisters and brother were very happy and attentive to all the guests, that my grandfather Toño built a makeshift bar to serve drinks, and even my grandfather Carlos, who never drank, got drunk that night celebrating the wedding of his first-born daughter, his little girl, his nurse.

Circa 1980s. When my grandmother became the temporary caregiver for me and my siblings, I imagine that, for her, it must have felt like being a mother all over again. The first set of grandchildren to run wild through her beautiful house, after so many years without any young kids to look after, after raising her own children and seeing them grow and become professional adults, she found herself once again giving away her magical, unconditional love to us.

Grandma Fina

Circa 1990s. There's a certain pride that fills my heart when I look at these pictures of my family. In this photo, their faces also carry that pride and love, that joy of knowing they are the living family tree. A beautiful moment in time captured here in this photograph.

Josefina Juarez

Chapter 1

Countless years have passed since Grandma Fina departed this world, but her memories still flood me daily like the rushing river that flows eternally in the imaginary of Macondo. She was much more than just a grandmother; she was a beacon of tenderness, a refuge of wisdom, and a pure soul that illuminated my existence in ineffable ways.

Growing up by her side was like living in a parallel world, a world in which time did not follow the rules imposed by the clock, but bent to her will, flowing slowly like a river of serene waters. The rains that soaked our garden were never a nuisance, but a divine blessing that revitalized the earth, and the sun that caressed us always had the gentleness of an old friend returning after a long time.

In that timeless world we shared, crime and fear were foreign terms, strangers who only dared to show their heads on the small TV screen, but never ventured to disturb our reality. Grandma Fina was the guardian of that paradise, with her arms always open and her eternal smile, ready to protect me from any storm that threatened to darken our days.

Her love was a bottomless ocean, an infinite river flowing from her generous heart into mine. She made me feel like the most precious treasure in her life, and every day was an adventure we shared together. She would take me to the park, where pigeons were messengers of ancient secrets, she would teach me to cook with recipes that had been passed down from generation to generation, and she would tell me stories of our ancestors that made me feel connected to a deep ancestral heritage.

Grandma Fina carried an umbrella with her, not only as a shield against inclement weather, but as a tangible symbol of her unwavering love and constant protection. That umbrella was a shelter she would deploy in times of rain, but also a metaphor for how she would always be there, ready to cover me with her love and care on the gray days of life.

When the day finally came when Grandma Fina departed this world, I shed no tears, and even today I wonder why. Perhaps I was too young to understand the magnitude of death, or maybe it was because I had a childlike faith that she would always be by my side, protecting me from the storms and onslaughts of the outside world.

However, with the passing of the years and the maturity that comes with time, I have come to understand how fortunate I was to have her in my life. She was my teacher in the school of kindness, my guide in the labyrinth of strength, and my example of how to love unconditionally. Her presence gave me a sense of belonging, and taught me that family is more than the blood that runs through our veins; it is the love and care we share.

Although Grandma Fina has departed, her legacy lives on in me, like a flame that never goes out and like the memories I treasure fondly. I am eternally grateful for the time we shared, for the world of love and kindness she created around me, and for the eternity of her presence in my heart. She was more than a grandmother; she was a magical story in my life, a chapter I will never forget as long as I breathe in this world.

Circa late 1990s. Pictured here are the two women that would end up shaping the world around me. From them, I learned many valuable lessons, such as the meaning of unconditional love, strength, leadership, sacrifice, self-respect, how to forgive, how to look at the bigger picture, and how to live a life with a sense of responsibility, to name a few.

A Special World

Chapter 2

Growing up next to Grandma Fina was an experience that immersed me in a world far removed from the rush and worries of the outside world. It was like living in a haven of time, a corner where the hours passed with the slowness of a nostalgic melody, and where the clock had hardly any relevance in our lives.

In that special world, the rain that fell on our garden was never a nuisance, but a blessing that enveloped us with its sweet scent of wet earth and reminded us of the vitality of nature. When the first drops hit the ground, Grandma Fina and I used to run to the porch and watch how the drops fell like liquid diamonds, creating circles in puddles and generating a musical rustle on the tin roof.

The sun, always warm and generous, seemed to greet us every morning like an old friend. Its golden rays caressed our skin and enveloped us with a sense of well-being that made us forget the worries of the outside world. It was as if the sun conspired with Grandma Fina to create a universe where happiness was the only language we understood.

In that corner of our world, crime and fear were distant words that only had a place in the news on the black and white television that occupied a corner of the living room.

Grandma Fina always protected us from those horrors, like a guardian keeping the demons of reality away. Her hugs were an impenetrable shield, and her words of encouragement were a balm that calmed any fears.

That special world I shared with Grandma Fina extended beyond the confines of our home, and as we walked through the neighborhood together, people greeted us with a warmth that reflected the close-knit community we were. Neighbors shared their stories, their secret recipes, and their life advice as if we were one big extended family. Everyone seemed to have been infected by Grandma Fina's kindness and welcoming spirit.

So, in that world where time lulled in the shadows of the trees and the rain was a celestial dance, Grandma Fina wove the tapestry of my childhood. Every day was a new chapter in a magical tale we shared, where magic and beauty were hidden in everyday details. As I grew up, that world became a treasure in my heart, a place I return to in my dreams and memories, searching for the peace and tenderness that only Grandma Fina knew how to give me.

Circa 1980s. After my grandma died, I would spend all my nights lying in bed, not being able to sleep, my face buried in the pillow. With my eyes closed, I would travel back to my childhood days and hold her hand again as I reimagined us walking under her umbrella to the pulpería. Doing this helped me mourn her death. Today, I am more than sure my grandmother, under my pillow, left me a verse.

Unconditional Love

Chapter 3

Grandma Fina was not only a presence in my life; she was the lighthouse that illuminated my days and the inspiration that guided my steps. Her love for me was an unfathomable ocean, a river that flowed from the depths of her soul into mine, and enveloped me with the warmth of an eternal embrace.

Often, we would venture together to the nearby park, where tall trees whispered millennia-old stories and birds shared their secrets in enigmatic melodies. Grandma Fina would gently hold my hand, and as we walked, she would teach me to appreciate the beauty of nature around us. For her, every flower, every leaf, was a work of art worthy of admiration, and she transmitted her love for life to me with every step we took.

In the kitchen, Grandma Fina displayed her culinary magic. Every dish she prepared was a delight that seemed to have the taste of nostalgia and tradition. She taught me to mix ingredients with love and to cook from the heart, passing on recipes that had been a legacy from generation to generation. Her expert hands and loving smile were the secret ingredient that made every meal a feast of emotions.

But what I treasure most are the stories Grandma Fina used to tell me before bedtime. Sitting under the stars twinkling in the night sky, she would narrate stories of our ancestors with a passion that turned them into epic tales. Her words were like a bridge connecting the past and the present, and made me feel part of a tradition that transcended time.

She carried an umbrella with her, a symbol of her love and protection. When she opened that umbrella on rainy days, it not only sheltered us from the raindrops falling from the sky, but also created a sanctuary where the outside world was suspended. It was as if we were in a sacred place, protected by Grandma Fina's tenderness and affection.

When the day came for Grandma Fina to leave this world, I

shed no tears, and I still don't know why. Perhaps it was because, in my innocence, I believed that she would never leave us completely, that her love would continue to be a shield against the storms of life. But over the years, I have come to understand that her love and legacy live on in me, like a fire that never goes out.

The unconditional love that Grandma Fina gave me is a beacon that lights my path, a compass that guides me in times of uncertainty. Through her teachings and example, she showed me how to be kind, strong and how to love unconditionally. Her legacy is a treasure that I treasure deep within me, and I know that her influence will live on in our family for generations to come. Grandma Fina was not only a grandmother; she was a gift of love and wisdom that will continue to inspire us to be better people, to value family and to live with an open heart. Her presence lives on in every corner of my life, and her everlasting love is the light that never goes out in my path.

A Lasting Legacy

Chapter 4

Although Grandma Fina has departed, her legacy lives on in every corner of my life like a river of memories that flows with the same vitality as her memories. And, among all those memories, there is one that stands out as a special treasure: the Sundays when all my aunts and uncles would gather at our house, creating a magical corner where family became the epicenter of life.

I vividly remember those Sundays, when the aroma of chicken soup with coconut milk would take over all my senses. Grandma Fina, with her loving eyes and expert hands, would prepare this dish with care. The fresh coconut became a delicacy, and its water was poured into a pitcher, refreshing like a spring in the middle of the tropical heat. As we waited for the soup to be ready, the sound of laughter and shared stories filled the house, creating a symphony of joy that echoed in my heart.

Those Sunday lunches were a sacred ritual, a celebration of family unity that Grandma Fina valued above all else. We all sat around the table, and the stories of our lives were intertwined with grandparents' anecdotes and Grandma Fina's teachings. It was as much a feast for the spirit as it was for the palate.

Each of my uncles brought his own spark of personality to the gathering. There was laughter, friendly discussion and shared advice. Grandma Fina, with her ancestral wisdom, acted as the epicenter of that effervescent world, guiding us with her love and patience. Her soft voice and tender gaze were the link that united the whole family in a network of love and complicity.

After those lunches, we felt renewed and strengthened by Grandma Fina's love and family unity. It was as if those moments charged us with energy and hope to face the week ahead.

Today, when I close my eyes and let the memories wash over me, I can feel the taste of fresh coconut on my lips and the aroma of the chicken soup with coconut milk that filled the house. I can hear the laughter of my uncles, and I can feel the loving presence of Grandma Fina, who continues to be the guiding light of our family.

Grandma Fina taught us that family is a treasure to be cherished and nurtured. Her legacy lives on in each of us, in the values we share and in the love that unites us. Although she is no longer physically present, her spirit lives on in every Sunday lunch, in every shared smile and in every loving embrace. Her influence is everlasting, like a song that never fails to play in the depths of our hearts, reminding us of the importance of family and the power of unconditional love.

But the magic of that special world was not only due to Grandma Fina. Behind her was Grandpa Carlos Zúñiga, a type of man not easily found in today's world. He dedicated his life to his family and his work, and his unconditional love and support were the foundation of our home.

Grandpa Carlos was a man of principle, the kind you rarely see in this modern era. He was always there for Grandma Fina and for us, his grandchildren. He worked tirelessly to provide for the family, but never let his work interfere with his commitment to us.

Together with Grandma Fina, they created an environment where love and unity were non-negotiable. They taught us fundamental values such as honesty, responsibility and respect for others. Grandpa Carlos was the quiet but wise man who always had a word of wisdom in difficult moments.

His supportive presence and love for Grandma Fina were palpable, and his legacy lives on in our family. Grandma Fina and Grandpa Carlos Zuniga were the perfect example of a mutually supportive couple who instilled lasting values in future generations. Although they are no longer physically present, their influence and love lives on in our hearts and in every aspect of our lives.

The Guava Tree

Chapter 5

That guava tree in my Grandma Fina's house. It was my playground, my refuge, my everything. I literally grew up in those branches, spending endless afternoons jumping from them, picking ripe guavas and waiting for Grandpa Carlos to come home from work.

Those afternoons were golden, so vivid in my mind, even now. I remember the excitement of shouting Grandpa's name when his bus arrived, and the joy of seeing him greet me. I remember the taste of those hand-picked guavas, sweet and juicy, bursting with flavor.

And I remember the smell of Grandma Fina's cooking, wafting from the kitchen, calling us home for dinner. Those dinners were always a feast, with Grandma's delicious homemade flour tortillas, refried beans and all the other delicacies she prepared.

The flavors were so familiar, so comforting, so uniquely hers. I can still taste them if I close my eyes. But it was that guava tree that defined those afternoons, that made them magical. It was a place of infinite possibilities, where I could be whoever I wanted to be, where I could escape the world and just be a kid.

I remember climbing to the top, feeling the breeze on my face and looking out into the world, feeling that anything was possible. And when Grandma Fina called us to dinner, I would jump out of that tree, landing with a soft thump on the soft earth below, and run inside, my stomach growling with hunger. It was a simpler time, a time of innocence and wonder. A time when that guava tree was the center of my world.

Now, as an adult, I realize how much that tree meant to me, how it shaped me, how it gave me a sense of belonging and home. And even though that little tree is gone, felled by someone who didn't understand its value, its memory lives on in me. That guava tree will always be a part of who I am, a reminder of the golden afternoons of my childhood and the love and warmth of my Grandma Fina's home.

My sister Gissel is the original rebel; she always stood up for what she thought was right, and she was usually right. In her fearless spirit, I found inspiration to be brave like her, even if it meant going against the current of my parents' expectations. When she was in Shenandoah Senior High, she used to take typewriting classes and bring home her school typewriter. She would let me play with it, and we would talk and laugh and type little notes together just to practice typing. Today, I own close to thirty typewriters myself, and I thank Gissel for bringing hers home from school back then.

Gissel

When my parents moved to New York City in 1974, my sister was just two years old. In this picture, my sister is dancing with my cousin Enock, son of my aunt Clarita, my dad's older sister.

Gissel's Birth

In a quiet corner of the city of La Lima, Cortez in a hospital enveloped in the warm afternoon breeze, an event was taking place that would change the course of the lives of those who witnessed it. It was a singular day, full of mystery and expectation, and the protagonists, full of emotion, waited anxiously in the waiting room, oblivious to the magical twist that was about to happen.

In the memory of those present, the whisper of a confidant who approached the ear of the father, who waited nervously, is preserved. The doctor, pronouncing the words, painted on his face a smile full of light: "Your daughter has been born, your firstborn, a beautiful baby girl." Gissel was born, the child who was to transform their lives, and the excitement in the room was beyond description.

The father, who had traveled countless roads, overcome obstacles and immersed himself in a thousand adventures, experienced an instant metamorphosis. Tears of joy welled up in his eyes, and his smile was brighter than the sun itself. His daughter was born! It was an unimaginable miracle, but there she was, a gift of destiny they could never have imagined.

At her side, sharing her enthusiasm, was Esperanza, the mother. Her face radiated a special light as she celebrated this magical moment with her father. Together, they had looked forward to this day, and with Gissel's arrival, their family was complete in a way that only fate could have planned.

In that world of uncertainty and anticipation that is nine months of waiting, the crowning moment finally arrived. The parents celebrated with friends and family, toasting with beer and celebrating the arrival of this new life into the world.

Little Gissel, with her angelic face, inherited her mother's beauty and her father's strength. She was a gift from the universe, and everyone knew that her future would be dazzling. Would she be a prodigious athlete, an engineering genius or a talented artist? No one could predict, but everyone was convinced she would be a star in whatever path she chose. When they returned to the bunkhouse, where the grandparents,

Josefina and Carlos were anxiously waiting, with the nursery and crib ready for Gisselita, they rushed to embrace the new parents and meet the family's first granddaughter.

Friends and neighbors joined in the celebration. Beer chilled in a corner, music filled the air and joy spread like a contagion. That party, which seemed to have no end, was a tribute to the arrival of Gissel, a little girl who had brought joy and hope to all.

The godparents showed up with gifts and good wishes. The night progressed, but no one wanted it to end. Hugs, laughter and singing filled the air. On that day, Gissel was not only born in the hospital, but also in the hearts of everyone present.

Life had taken a magical and beautiful turn with the arrival of Gissel, a little girl who would become the light of their lives, a reason to smile every day. The celebration continued, and as they looked to the future with hope, they knew that Gissel would be an extraordinary child and that her story was just beginning. In this story, the love and joy of Esperanza and the father would be the solid foundation on which Gissel would build her own path in the charming city of San Pedro Sula.

Pictured here is Gissel, after one of her school performances. The year is 1979.

Ever since my sister was a little girl, my parents made sure to encourage her to participate in all types of art activities happening at school. My sister was inclined to sing; she started in elementary school and high school and even had her own agent. More than once, I remember all of us going to the Calle Ocho Street festival in Little Havana to see her perform.

1974, New York City. My dad used to always work out: push-ups, sit-ups, and pull-ups. He would create a workout session out of anything around him, like a chair or couch. He was always lifting weights or lifting something heavy. If he didn't have anything heavy, he would use one of us for lifting. We used to love that.

Mis padres con mi hermanita en el brazo de mi papa, mi madre con una blusa blanca partiendo un cake. 1974

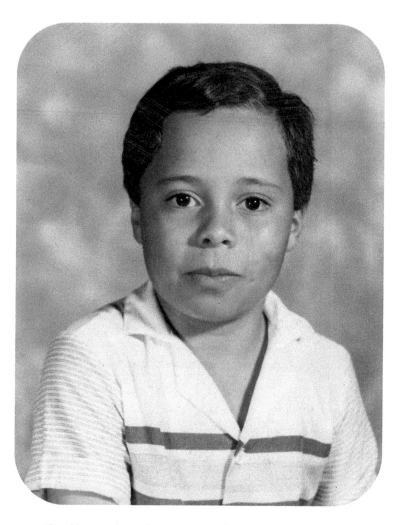

If I could say something to the younger version of me in this photograph, it would be that it all worked out, that we survived, and that I am your future. At that age, it was difficult to see or know how things would unfold, but through the years, you learn to enjoy the journey and go through it all with faith, knowing things will work out one way or another. Fears will come and go, and every lesson learned and unlearned about what love truly is will become clearer as you get older. Life is a journey of self-knowledge, and even though we found ourselves alone at times, the universe had a plan for us all along. Here we are today with an enormous family, sons and daughters, an artistic career, and a happy heart that makes us sleep like babies at night.

Mandito

New York City, 1975. In New York, my dad worked as a cook. He had learned all about cooking during his time working on the cargo ship through Europe. In New York cooking jobs were easy to find, but little did he know that in the coming years and for the rest of his life, he would use the carpentry and masonry skills he learned from his father.

Manhattan, New York, 1975

One afternoon in January 1975, my father, Oscar Fuentes, overwhelmed by memories, was working as a cook in a New York restaurant with his brother-in-law, Armando Montes, husband of his older sister, Clarita. My mother was rocking in a chair, where she would soon begin to feel labor pains. It was a snowy afternoon when, at the restaurant, the phone rang for my dad with the news that it was time to leave for the hospital. Oscar and his brother-in-law ran out into the cold and relentless snow to the train station.

By all accounts, I was born on one of the heaviest snow days in New York history. It was in the afternoon, January 25, 1975. In those years, my parents had overstayed their tourist visas and, as a result, were in an illegal immigration situation, as well as having difficulty speaking English properly. This hindered their ability to properly complain at Roosevelt Hospital when they noticed my left hand wrapped and stained with blood.

Apparently, one of the nurses had put the serum not in my vein, but on my skin, and the fluid burned the top of my hand. To this day, 40 years later, the scar is still there. I remember my mom always told me that when I grew up, the scar would hide, but it never did, since I was always a short guy.

1975, New York City. Pictured here is my mother holding me as a newborn baby, with my sister standing with us. I can't imagine how difficult it must've been for my mom to live in New York with a newborn baby and a three-year-old toddler, with my dad working long hours at the restaurant. I know she had support from my aunt Clarita, who also lived in New York with her husband, and my dad's older brother Reynaldo and his wife, but it must've still been difficult for my mom. Those were days long gone, belonging to another time, a time that belonged to my parents.

Barracón # 1883

That's where we all lived, where we grew up together. My aunts and uncles, they were all children.

My sister Gissel was two years old and I was only eight months old.

I had a red scar on the top of my hand and Grandma Fina and Grandpa Carlos took care of me with a strong affection.

I had an allergy to the milk they gave me and I would vomit after drinking Pepe. My grandmother always warned my aunts:

"Beware of making that child vomit or I'll give you all an earful!" and my aunts Julia and Lupe would give me the bottle with such care.

However, when they started to burp me very carefully, I would vomit once again. My grandparents finally took me to Dr. Boto, a local pediatrician, and he finally gave me a remedy for the vomiting.

Then I could drink my milk and my young aunts Lupe and Julia could feed me and play with me without worrying about getting in trouble with my grandmother.

As I grew up, I became close to a neighbor of my grandparents named Santiago. He was only about a year and a half old, and my Aunt Julia tells me that whenever I saw him, I would get so excited and run to him yelling, "Tatayo! Tatayo! Look, a louse!" pointing to my hair to let him know I had lice.

And I would embarrass all my aunts, since now everyone knew we had lice in the barracks.

Julia also remembers that my Uncle Alonzo was very close to me and Gissel, especially Gissel, because she was the first niece in the family.

Eventually, we all moved from the barracón to the current house near the entrance to the Rivera Hernández neighborhood, where many other stories unfolded for each of us.

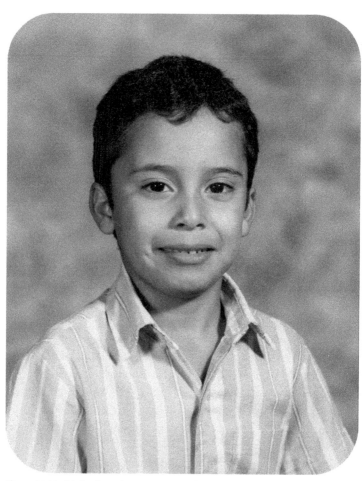

Circa mid-80s. My brother is three years younger than me, and for the early years of our lives, he was my little brother. However, as we got older, he became taller than me and, I want to say, matured faster than I did. Today, my brother is a hero of mine. I look up to him and admire him as a person. He is an excellent son to our parents and a wonderful, loving father. My brother always inspires me, and he is someone that I love and respect dearly.

Toñito

2021, Miami, Florida. This picture captures the time we celebrated my parents' 50th wedding anniversary. It was so nice for all of us to meet in Miami, take pictures together, document, and celebrate my parents' love journey.

Carlos Antonio Fuentes (My Younger Brother)

My younger brother, Carlos Antonio Fuentes, somehow had it easy with my parents for being the youngest of the three. It is as if my parents, with my sister Gissel, their first born, tried to mold her with the parenting style my grandparents used with them, not knowing that my sister has the spirit of an untamed wild lion, and so, I am sure my parents learned and unlearned many lessons about parenting and what it means to raise a child born with her own personality already fully developed. When I was born, it must have been for my parents as their second chance to try out all the different parenting skills they had learned with my sister and in me they found a pacifist child, and in comparison to my sister, and to my parents, I must have seemed extremely relaxed and calm. By the time Carlos was born, I think my parents had given up all parenting efforts and pretty much allowed him to do whatever he wanted. I'm exaggerating here, of course. Joking aside, I admire my brother Carlos. I am inspired by the way he behaves like a loving son to our parents. He is an excellent father to his two children, Daniel and Valeria, and a loyal and loving companion to Belkis. My brother was always better at everything he did. Dad used to be a Bruce Lee fan and so he managed to keep us in karate school throughout our youth, actually almost 18 years, and of the three of us, Carlos was the only one who ended up finding a lifelong career in the martial arts. Between my sister, he and I, we had close to a hundred trophies from all the tournaments we competed in, Dad even built shelves along an entire wall for us to display them. Looking at all those trophies, for my dad, it must have been a representation of his efforts as a father who provided an athletic outlet for his children. If I had to describe my brother in three words, I would choose: resilient, motivated and committed.

Circa late 80s. Silver Bluff Elementary was one of the elementary schools my brother and I attended. My sister went to a different school; she was in middle school. These elementary school years were a lot of fun for us. We played a lot together. My sister was very kind to us, a very loving and attentive sister. During those days, we had a pretty tight routine of going to school and then going to karate school until dinner time. This routine stayed with us for 18 years until we were young adults.

Miami

Circa 1990s. My grandmother had a deep sense of humility and compassion. In her simple, selfless, generous spirit, she had a visceral sense of understanding and made everyone feel loved and appreciated.

The Farewell

I remember that day as if it were a slow-motion movie. I see myself saying goodbye to my grandmother, standing in front of her house. The suitcases were already in the trunk of the cab. My grandfather Carlos was sitting in the front with the driver, in the back seat were my mom, Gissel, Toño and me, looking at my grandmother through the window. We were both crying, looking intensely into each other's eyes with that unique love of grandmother and grandson. The image of my granny grew smaller and smaller as the cab slowly drove away towards the airport.

I would cry out her name through childish tears, knowing that this lady we were leaving behind loved her more than my own mother. My mind was filled with beautiful memories with her, my cousins Jenny and Carolina, and my aunts. All those nights when I would fall asleep to the smell of Vicks Vaporub that she would put on my chest, and I would fall asleep in her arms, feeling that with her by my side, nothing bad could happen.

That separation marked the beginning of my new stage away from Honduras and my new life in Miami.

Circa mid-80s. This picture captured a very happy moment in our childhood. We shared many happy memories with our cousins in Miami, getting together, playing, hanging out, celebrating birthdays, and other special occasions. Pictures like this one are plentiful in the photo album of our memories. Here, we see my cousin Junior wearing a black shirt and smiling. He passed away a while ago. Junior was the one who welcomed me to Miami when I arrived from Honduras. He made me feel welcome, took me under his wings, showed me how to breakdance, and took me everywhere on the handlebars of his BMX. Even into my adulthood, my cousin was always very special to me. I love this photograph.

Bonding Ties

The sun was setting on the horizon as the plane descended towards Miami. My heart was beating with a mix of excitement and nervousness as I anticipated meeting my cousins from my father's side of the family for the first time. During my childhood, most of my memories were intertwined with my mother's family in Honduras. Their warmth and constant presence in my life made them the cornerstone of my world.

Arriving at my new home in Miami, I found myself in a world that was both familiar and foreign. Although I hadn't yet met the cousins from my father's side who lived in Miami, I was already acquainted with the Fuentes cousins from Honduras. The dynamics with my father's side of the family were different. It was typical for the mother's side of the family to be more involved with the children, but here, interactions were less frequent by default. Nevertheless, every moment with my father's cousins revealed layers of love and unity that transcended any differences.

I discovered unique traditions and cultural nuances that distinguished my father's family. From lively gatherings full of laughter to quiet moments of shared stories, each experience deepened my connection with them. Our bond grew stronger as we navigated the initial adjustments, forging memories that would become cherished chapters in our family's history.

Reflecting on those times, I realized that Miami held a treasure trove of memories with my father's side of the family. Those shared moments taught me that family is not defined by proximity or frequency of interactions; it's about the love and unity that bind us together. My time in Miami was more than just living with cousins; it was about bonding ties and embracing the richness of diverse family dynamics.

The town of Riolindo held a special place in my heart, with its beautiful, noisy river where we used to bathe and play. Those moments by the river with my cousins, Enoch, Fabiola, and Gabriela, were etched in my memory, carrying the joy and freedom of childhood adventures that I always cherished.

Growing up in Miami, I spent a lot of time with my aunt Zulema, who worked at the Bacardi Building on Biscayne Boulevard at 21st. Her children, Vanessa and Miguelito, were younger than us, but we shared countless laughs and created cherished memories together. I vividly remember celebrating birthdays with them, blowing out cake candles, and capturing these moments of joy in photographs that I hold dear to this day.

Ultimately, my parents had to return to Honduras due to their illegal immigration status, leaving me alone to navigate life in Miami. During this time, my aunt Zulema became a significant presence in my life. She got to know a teenage version of me, witnessing my journey as I became a young man with a job, attending school, finishing high school, and applying to an art college. Her support and understanding during this period were invaluable, and to this day, I am deeply grateful for her presence in my life.

Through the years, both my parents finally became American citizens, eventually retiring from work, and figuring out a way to live more than half of the year in Honduras and a few months in Miami mainly for their doctor appointments. Everyone eventually grew older, and some even passed away. In my heart, I can feel the lingering saddened memory of the loss of family members I loved so deeply, such as my grandparents Toño, Nena, and Fina, my cousin Junior who took me under his wings in the early 80s and introduced me to a whole new way of life in a breakdancing America, and my aunt Miriam and uncle Alonso who I remember them hanging out together in Miami at our family gathering at our house. And most recently, the loss of my uncle Marcos, the oldest of the Fuentes uncles.

Circa late 90s. Colonia La Planeta, Honduras. We are sitting outside the porch of the house we used to live in La Colonia Planeta. In this picture, you see my dad and his older sister, my aunt Clarita, before I flew back to Miami. I believe my visit to Honduras that time was close to a month long.

Gerardo

Uncle Gerardo and ET

I remember this story as a tale interwoven in the folds of time, steeped in nostalgia and wrapped in the magical realism of life itself. It all began when my uncle Gerardo embarked on the mission of preparing me for the entrance exam to the technical high school in San Pedro Sula, in those days when adolescence seemed like a horizon full of questions and promises.

My uncle Gerardo, a man with a generous heart, deployed his efforts with admirable tenacity to instill knowledge and discipline in me. However, I, in my rebellious youth, was never a focused child, at least not in the way required to pass that crucial test. My mind flew among the butterflies of imagination, while he tried to anchor it in the pages of books and in the possible questions that might assail me in the future.

But my uncle Gerardo did not only leave his mark on my life at that moment. Five or seven years earlier, he took me to the movies in San Pedro to see the premiere of Steven Spielberg's *ET*. I remember the joy it gave me when I knew we were going to the movies, when I realized that my uncle had chosen me to share that unique moment. It was just him and me, immersed in a crowd that disappeared before the magic of the screen. As the *ET* story unfolded before our eyes, I experienced a special connection with my uncle, as if we were suspended in time, between two alien worlds, one real and the other full of dreams.

My uncle Gerardo, in his youth, had been an Olympic athlete, capable of amazing physical feats, and I remember seeing photographs of him defying gravity with a long pole, overcoming obstacles that looked like something out of fairy tales. To me, in my childhood mind, he was a true hero, despite being my mother's younger brother. He was a beacon of wonder and awe amidst the vast ocean of my childhood.

Years passed and eventually my parents took us back to Miami, leaving San Pedro Sula and my uncle Gerardo behind. I lost touch with him, and I blame myself, as I was swept up in the course of growing up in a new city, where school life and new friendships kept me busy. Although I was born in New York, my early years were spent with my grandparents in Honduras, and without my uncle by my side, I was forced to give in to that whirlwind and become a young man who always carried the memory of my heroic and special uncle, Gerardo Zúniga, in his heart.

Circa early to mid-1990s, Miami, FL. When my uncle Gerardo arrived in Miami, he came with a lot of work experience. He knew how to work with his hands and was a master carpenter. I remember he had a big job working on a mansion off of Pinetree Drive in Miami Beach, working with oversized wooden doors. He was so proud to have completed the job, and the owners praised his fine woodworking skills. Today, he is still the same happy uncle we have always known. I want to say that the bond my sister, brother, and I share with my uncle Gerardo is a very unique and special one.

Circa 1980s. I was very young when my uncle was out playing soccer in his young adulthood. I remember him on the field, being very sporty. As I got older, and we visited Honduras from Miami, I always remember my uncle waiting for us at the customs area because he worked for customs at the airport. Our luggage was always ready, and entering the country was easy because of my uncle. My uncle was a businessman, a very respected individual, a loving father to my cousins, a loving husband, and very loving with my grandparents. My uncle's loss was a very painful blow to all of us in our family. I know that right now he is next to my grandmother and my aunt Miriam, catching up on the things they need to catch up on. I know the three of them will continue to guide us from above.

Uncle Alonso

Alonso (Carlos A. Zuniga Juárez)

When I was a child, and almost all my aunts still lived there, in my grand-parents Zuniga's house, there also lived two cousins of my grandfather Carlos: Oscar and Hector. I don't remember which of the two had cut a finger on one of their hands once when they pounded fresh water co-conuts to accompany those family Sunday lunches. Every time I was served that fresh coconut water, I remembered Hector's poor finger. I loved these two cousins of my grandfather's very much; they helped me a lot and took care of me a lot. When my grandmother sent them to buy wood for the stove, I begged her to let me go with them. At home, errands were done on a bicycle or on a moped. I remember once when Hector and I went out in the afternoon to buy bread and sugar at one of the grocery stores in Calpules, I was sitting on the back rack of the bicycle. We had already crossed the entire neighborhood when Hector asked me:

Hector: *"Mandito, do you want to stop by the field for a little while to see your uncle Alonso play?"*

I always listened to Hector talk about my uncles, how good they played soccer and now it was finally my chance to see them in ac-tion.

Me: *"Yeah, man, come on!"*

In those days, my uncles played soccer and it was common to see them play with that group of people that came from all the nearby colonies to play different games. Hector took me to the field where they played. There were my uncles Gerardo and Alonso, Quique Carillon, Bonerjes, the Captain and Beto, some of the best players in town. They were part of that group of friends who gathered every weekend to enjoy soccer and camaraderie.

Spectators filled the makeshift bleachers, cheering on their teams with passion. The tension in the air was noticeable as the players prepared for the game.

I waved to my uncles from afar and they responded, "Mandi-to!"

The referee blew his whistle, kicking off the match. The ball was rolling from one side of the field to the other, with Quique Carillon showing his skill in the midfield, controlling the pace of the game.

Gerardo, known for his speed and agility, was slipping between opposing defenders, looking for an opportunity to score. The captain led his team with determination, organizing the defense and launching quick attacks towards the opposing goal. Beto, the goalkeeper, was making impressive saves, keeping his goal unbeaten.

The match was tight, with both teams struggling to dominate the game. But it was in a moment of brilliance that Alonso, up front, took control of the ball. With a series of feints and dribbles, he left his markers behind and planted himself in front of goal. With a powerful shot, the ball soared through the air and into the net, scoring a spectacular goal.

The field erupted in joy as the fans celebrated my uncle Alonso's goal. His teammates and Gerardo ran towards him to congratulate him, while the opponents recognized the genius of the goal. It was a moment of glory for Alonso and the whole team, which will remain etched in the memory of everyone present for a long time to come. But my uncle Alonso also had many symbolic goals in life, goals, blessings with his beautiful family, Estela, his two daughters and two sons, and in the middle of time, his grandchildren. Goal and blessing for him was also to have been born from the marriage of his loving parents, my grandparents, who always had an unconditional love for this whole Zuniga family that inspires love. Today all of us Zuniga's know very well that for us, the greatest goal and blessing was my uncle Alonso, with his generosity and dedication to his family and friends, with his fatherly sincerity and that of a son and brother who always shone with a light guided by God.

Relics of the Heart

Circa late 80s or early 90s. In this photograph, the first person you see is my aunt Miriam. She looks so youthful, healthy, and happy, smiling. My aunt Julia sits next to her with her eyes closed, and standing by the wall is my mother, also attentively listening.

Aunts

Circa late 80s or early 90s. Honduras. I know my aunt Miriam adored her son Juan Carlos. That love was the very reason why she went to the U.S. to find a better opportunity. If she could only see the beautiful example of success her son is today, a beloved medical doctor and owner of a hospital building that bears our last name.

Cheers To Our Brave Guardians!

Eldy: [Raising her wine glass] *Do you remember that scary day?*

Lupe: [Nodding] *How could I forget it! It was a scare that left us all trembling.*

Gloria: [Taking a sip of wine] *What exactly happened?*

Aide: [J oining the conversation] *Oh yes, didn't I tell you boys can be so naughty sometimes?*

Eldy: [Laughing] *Yes, but this was no mere child's play. It was a real danger.*

Lupe: [Looking outside] *I remember seeing that boy running towards us, crying and screaming.*

Gloria: [With intrigue] *And what happened next?*

Aide: [Continuing the story] *Julia and Miriam jumped like lightning towards him, they didn't even look to see if cars were coming!*

Eldy: [Nodding] *It was an incredible act of bravery. I don't know how they crossed that street so fast.*

Lupe: [Wistfully] *But the most important thing is that they got there in time to protect him.*

Gloria: [Emotional] *Wow, sounds like a really intense moment.*

Aide: [Nodding] *It was. Miriam showed impressive bravery in standing up to the cab driver.*

Eldy: [Raising her glass] *To our amazing sisters, who were and are always* *there to protect us!*

Lupe: [Joining in the toast] *Cheers to that!*

Gloria: [Raising her glass] *Cheers to our brave guardians!*

[Aide, Eldy, Lupe and Gloria clink their glasses and continue enjoying their wine, remembering that day full of emotions.]

Circa 1990s. Miami, FL. In this picture, you see my mother and her sisters Julia Lupe, Aide, and her son, little Arthur Smith, who ended up becoming a coach for college football in West Virginia.

Circa 1990s. Miami, FL. Pictured here are my aunt Miriam and my aunt Julia.

Julia and Miriam

1981, Calpules, Honduras. Thursday 11:30 AM. That day I was walking home from elementary school to my grandmother's house. I was walking down the street that led directly to the Rivera Hernandez neighborhood and was approaching the main street. As I was walking, I was playing with some pebbles of gravel, when suddenly a bus passed by and I threw a pebble at one of the wheels, causing the pebble to bounce in the air. As I was a child, I laughed and found it amusing. Then I saw a white Volkswagen cab approaching. I prepared the small stone in the palm of my hand, walked slowly, waiting for the cab to come closer, and when it passed me, I quickly threw the pebble at the tire, which bounced off the hubcap of the wheel, producing a very loud metallic sound.

The car continued to move forward, I looked back and the car stopped. Then I saw the reverse lights come on and it started backing rapidly towards me. That's when I started running in horrible fear, screaming as loud as I could:

GRANNY! GRANNY! I kept running and screaming for my life. I was already directly across the street and I kept screaming and running.

On the other side of the street, in the shade of the porch of the house, rocking in hammocks, were my aunts, Yamile, Lupe, Eldy, Julia and Miriam. Through the noise of the busy street, they heard my six-year-old voice screaming for help. Julia and Miriam ran out of the house, in their jean shorts, with such speed, I don't even know how they crossed that street without looking to see if there were cars coming from either side. The next thing I knew, my Aunt Julia was hugging me and I was crying uncontrollably in her arms.

The cab stopped 10 feet away, the driver got out and just stared at us. "What's wrong with you, you crazy motherfucker? Watch out you touch this kid or I'll kill you!" Julia shouted hugging me. The man unbuckled his gun from his waistband, and before he could aim it at us, my Aunt Miriam appeared behind us, pushed us forcefully out of his way and onto the grass, and looked at him with fearless eyes.

"If you're going to shoot someone, shoot me," she said tapping her chest with her open right hand.

The man immediately lowered his gun and started complaining that I was the one who threw a rock at his car and broke his back window, and that....

"He's just a kid, what the hell are you doing, chasing him with your car? Are you crazy?" said Miriam, interrupting the man.

The cab driver, frustrated, got back in his car and drove off. The three of us crossed the street while Julia carried me in her arms, where my other aunts waited, relieved and crying, hugging and kissing me.

Circa 1990s. In this photograph, you see my mother, my aunt Aide, who is pregnant with my little cousin Arthur, and next to them is my grandaunt, sister of grandma Fina. I remember my mom bringing me along to her visits with them and listening to them talk while I drank soda with sweets and just hung out with them. I remember the car they're leaning against. I can even remember the light of the day captured in this photo.

Circa 1980s. In this picture, we see my aunt Rosita and my aunt Clarita sitting on a sofa in my grandparents' house in Colonia San Cristobal. I remember that same sofa, where I used to sit and play with my cousins. I remember that house so clearly—all the rooms, the first floor, the second floor, the living room, and the back patio. I remember my two aunts very clearly, always kind and loving, and happy, always very happy. I am so lucky to have them and their sisters Patricia and Zulema in my life, and my father was so lucky to have them as sisters.

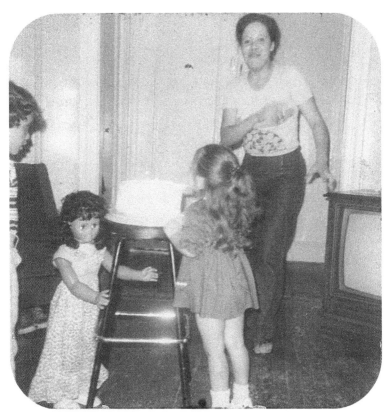

Circa 1973, New York City. In this photograph, you see my mother dancing. My sister and my cousin Junior are also in the picture. She looks so happy dancing in New York in 1973.

1998, Colonia San Cristobal, Honduras. In this photo, I am holding one of my father's roosters. When I went to Honduras in 1998 after Hurricane Mitch, to help with anything needed after the flood, I spent my days between our house in Colonia La Planeta and my grandfather's back patio in San Cristobal. Before the hurricane hit, my dad's main concern was making sure his apiary was above ground and that the roosters wouldn't drown in the flood. He owned about 80 roosters plus a good number of hens and chicks. My dad used to train these roosters for local cockfights. He was mindful about keeping all their areas clean with fresh sawdust and the birds well-fed and vaccinated.

The Cock Fight

I once attended a cock fight in Honduras. Many men waited for the cock-fighting circus to arrive. Eager owners gave rigorous training to their best roosters all year. People respected those owners, who were known for their prime fighting cocks.

On the small, seasoned patio where the event was held, one corner awaited the arrival of the cocks' cages. Inside roosters insulted each other with their songs. While the fighting roosters screamed their cock-a-doodle songs, people moved onto the patio, the home of the humble man who offered to build the fight ring and host the event.

The ring was built in the center of his patio. Surrounding it were wooden stools and chairs he made. The ring consisted of long strips of plywood around a circular frame. The floor was covered with sawdust, chips of cedar, and a dusting of pine.

In the corner opposite the roosters sat the humble man's wife, a passive woman, similar to many who lived in the village. She stood behind a wooden counter selling oranges, tropical fruit, and beer. The fanatic cock fighters drank so much beer, it seemed the event would never start.

When the beer was finally consumed and the cock fighters were all drunk, they lay on the floor. I imagined they were dead, because they lay without a word. Even the roosters were asleep. The only ones awake were the humble owner's wife and me.

She seemed angry, as if she were thinking, *The motherfucker! The fucking guy offers to host the event, builds a ring, gets drunk with his cock-fighting friends, and then forgets the whole thing!*

Grabbing an empty beer bottle, she slammed it against the six-foot concrete wall behind her. At the sound of the bottle exploding, the men woke up like killer bees snapping out of their daily work in the hive when someone hit it with a rock.

Immediately, her husband got into the center of the ring and said, "Beinvenidos sean todos los galleros que se encuentran aqui presente. Mucha suerte, y que empieze la pelea de gallos! Hijos de puta!"

The cock fighters cheered loudly, and two jumped into the ring carrying roosters. They shook hands and let the roosters see each other. The birds, instantly ready to fight, were beautiful, more elegant than eagles.

The men in the ring signaled each other and tossed their birds into the air, as the audience cheered. In the corner where the cages waited, the roosters seemed to meditate on the crowd's noise, but they were totally quiet.

For a moment, time seemed to freeze. We all sat motionless, our mouths open, staring at the birds in the air. They seemed to float three or four feet above the center of the ring, stabbing at each other. When they connected and disconnected, sharp spurs pierced each other's bodies.

For a few moments, they battled in the air, then one landed on the floor head first, almost dead, spitting blood. Scarlet red stained the yellow sawdust covering the floor.

The victor glided down to the floor with elegance and grace, creating gusts of wind by flapping his wings and sending sawdust everywhere in a cloud that blocked all visibility. The crowd was totally silent, as the victor folded his wings and sang his victory song. The cocks in the cages added their voices to the chaos. The audience returned to normal. The host's wife just received another keg of beer, and all the men formed a line in front of the wooden counter. I found a homemade stool and sat on it, knowing it would be awhile before the next match began.

Illustration by Crystal Garcia from the Zine, 'The Cock Fight,' written by me, Oscar Fuentes.

Circa 1970 or 1971. Picture of my father: Oscar Armando Fuentes Aguirre.

A Forgotten Friend

Oscar went for a bike ride. Gloria had decided to take the bus because she felt she was too old to ride a bike with Oscar.

The humble light blue house of Josefina, Gloria's mother, was six miles away from their home. They had both gone to visit the elderly, as it had been a while since they had last seen each other. Actually, Josefina had been sick for quite some time, and had come down with the flu very badly, and her knees had weakened, and the veins in her legs had also turned thick and blue, sometimes purple, but her daughter had gone to Oscar, and she was going to be fine.

Gloria had gone to nursing school and really knew how to handle the injection needle. Who knew exactly how many shots she had given people? Everyone in her neighborhood knew she was a certified nurse, and most of them had been to her house once or twice for an injection or two.

But now Gloria was inside her mother's house, the exact same house she had lived in since she was a little girl. Now, after fifty-something years, Gloria was in the old house and as she injected the antibiotic into her mother's left arm, Gloria thought about her childhood. She thought of the many little details etched in her memory. The walls of her mother's house, the old tile floor, the old high ceiling, her lost friends, her five sisters and two brothers, she thought of them as girls and boys, and she thought of time; how it had passed so quickly. Gloria thought of her three children and how each of them had started their family life. She thought of Oscar junior and his pregnant girlfriend, and the baby inside her womb.

"What are you thinking about, mami?" would ask Josefina.

"About my children. I'm thinking about my son." "They're beautiful, the three of them."

"Yes, I love them very much. "Yes, me too."

Gloria had already injected the antibiotic into her mother's arm and an hour had just passed since she had arrived at the old house.

"Look, here comes your husband."

"Where?"

"There." Josefina pointed her right arm out. Her left arm felt numb, with a constant electric shock of pain. Gloria looked out the windows and kept her eyes fixed on Oscar.

Oscar rode his bicycle up this small hill where the pavement of the main street had been laid, about fifty feet in front of Josefina's old house.

He kept going, maneuvering his bike and stopped it just inside the front door of the house. He got off the bike. He parked it under the tropical shade of an almond tree. He opened the front door slowly and entered under the tin roof of the front porch of the house.

Oscar entered the house through the front door feeling out of breath, his legs felt weak and sweat ran slowly down both sides of his forehead.

"You worried for a moment, my love." Gloria told her.

"Oh, I'm fine, my princess. It's been a while since I rode that bike." "I know." Gloria replied.

"Why don't you sit down and rest? I'll make you some good coffee." said Josefina.

"Thanks." replied Oscar.

He sat down on Josefina's old comfortable couch and let out a deep sigh. Then he let out a sigh.

Josefina cautiously took a step down onto the kitchen floor, which was on a lower level than the living and dining room floor, and began to heat the water for the coffee. Gloria and Oscar sat alone under the living room ceiling and looked at each other. Gloria smiled at him. He smiled back.

They both had puppy dog eyes and it was evident that the love was now stronger than ever.

After a while, Josefina came into the living room and handed Oscar his hot cup of good Honduran coffee. She sat down next to him on the couch. Gloria sat in one of the chairs at the dining room table, and the three of them talked and laughed for quite a while, and after five whole hours, the three of them felt tired, and Oscar and Gloria decided it was time to leave and head back to their little house.

They both kissed and hugged Josefina. Gloria gave her an extra hug, and they held each other tightly for a moment. Meanwhile, Oscar stayed outside the house, and under the cool tropical shade of Josefina's almond tree, and thought about his cockfighting roosters. He thought about training them some more, and he also thought about taking them to compete. All his life, Oscar had been a cockfighting fanatic. He owned seventy-two fighting cocks and sixty-three fine hens, also with a sigh he imagined himself working his hives back on brother-in-law Alonso's mountain property.

Finally, Gloria left her mother's house, and walked past the front gate, closing it behind her.

"Are you going to take the bus again?" Oscar asked her.

"Do you want me to go with you?" she asked.

"Only if you want to, but it's a long ride, maybe you should take the bus."

"Okay, I'll take the bus."

"I'll walk you to the bus stop."

They both started walking up the hill to the main street, and halfway up they turned and looked at the house, as if looking for Josefina, and she was there, standing behind the gate of her house and under the tin roof of her porch. Gloria and Oscar greeted her. Josefina waved back. They continued walking and started up the hill. They reached the main street and crossed it, making sure there were no cars coming from either side. They arrived at the bus stop. Oscar parked his bike to the side. He took Gloria's hand. Gloria took his. They kissed. They smiled. They waited for the bus to arrive.

After a moment of waiting, the bus finally arrived. Gloria got on, paid her fare. The bus began to move. She looked out the windows and looked for her husband. He was still there.
Standing, and waiting for her to look at him. She knew he would. And he had. They both looked at each other and smiled. Oscar waved. Gloria didn't. And their bus was now far away, heading toward their neighborhood.

Oscar unlocked the bicycle's parking pedal. He walked over and pushed the bike a little. Then he got on it. He started pedaling. And he was moving. Slowly gaining speed. He was going fast enough now. Fast enough to feel and hear the wind in his ear.

Between Josefina's house and the house Gloria and Oscar owned, there were six miles of sugar cane plantation. As he rode his bicycle, Oscar settled into a comfortable pedaling rhythm and worked at it without even realizing it. There was a pleasantly cool afternoon feeling in the air, and Oscar had not yet broken a sweat. He had rested his knees for five whole hours and they didn't feel weak; instead, they felt strong. His knees felt young and light.

He rode his bike down the narrow side of Main Street, which was dusty, and kept the road to himself there, making sure not to ride on the main road because this part of town had a bad reputation for drivers. Oscar senior had always preferred his horseback ride to the bus ride because he knew too many people, or should I say too many people knew him, and to avoid small talk, he would take the long way because the long way was lonely, quiet and peaceful.

Halfway from his house, in the middle of all that sugar cane plantation, Oscar stopped pedaling, and slowly, he and his bike stopped moving. It had been a long day full of nothing. No action. The sun looked good and giant and orange. He felt a little out of breath, but that was okay.

Right where Oscar stopped, right there in the middle of the road and the sugar cane, Oscar sighed deeply and thought about his children. Gloria's children were the same children Oscar would think of every time he thought of his own, and now Oscar thought of the youngest, Carlos Antonio Fuentes, who had recently moved out of the house, and into this simple little place he and his girlfriend had found in the foothills of Merendón Mountain.

"Damn it, Oscar, you made it." He would say to himself.

The orange Central American sun was slowly and majestically setting, and Oscar loved to catch the sun on its descent, and every day at this same time Oscar made sure to be outdoors, looking up at the sun, but he would never look directly at the sun, instead, he enjoyed contemplating the mix of colors in the Central American sky at this time in the afternoon, every day.

Today the sky looks prettier than yesterday, Oscar thought, and as he thought that, he noticed how it was getting dark and late, so he pushed his bicycle, got on it and continued riding home. The colors in the sky were fading, and the sky wasn't so pretty anymore, and Oscar knew it, but he still kept looking up as he rode the old horse. Then Oscar heard a voice. The voice came from behind him. Oscar turned his head and looked back. From behind him came someone riding a bicycle, but the person was too far away and Oscar could not see the face clearly.

"Oscar," the person called.

Oscar looked again and decided to stop completely. He turned around and waited for the person who had called his name twice. It was an old man who looked familiar, but he could not recognize who it was. Then, the man spoke to him.

Family Timeline

My Grandparents

Grandpa Toño (1921)

Grandma Nena (1924)

Grandpa Carlos (1926)

Grandpa Fina (1929)

My Parents

Gloria Esperanza
Fuentes Zuniga (1950)

Oscar Armando
Fuentes Aguirre (1953)

My Siblings and I

Gissel Fuentes (1972)

Oscar Fuentes Jr. (1975)

Toñito Fuentes (1978)

Aunts-Uncles Zuniga	My Aunts-Uncles Fuentes
Tio Alonso (1952)	Tio Marcos (1943)
Tia Aide (1954)	Tia Clara (1950)
Tia Miriam (1956)	Tio Rey (1948)
Tio Gerardo (1958)	Tia Rosita (1958)
Tia Lupe (1960)	Tio Salvador (1960)
Tia Julia (1963)	Tia Zulema (1962)
Tia Eldy (1966)	Tia Patricia (1967)

My Cousins Zuniga ——

Carolina Zuniga (1975)

Jenny Zuniga (1976)

Carlitos Zuniga (1978)

Alonso Zuniga (1981)

Juan Carlos Zuniga (1984)

Stephanie Smith (1986)

Gerardo Issac Zuniga (1986)

Mariela Escoto (1987)

Walter Escoto (1989)

Arturito Smith (1990)

Carlos Alonso Zuniga (1990)

Manuel Alejandro Gomez (1992)

Daniel Escoto (1994)

Jonathan Josue Zuniga (1994)

Nadia Gerardina Zuniga (1996)

Brayan Gerardo Zuniga (1998)

Carlos Manuel Gomez (2000)

Valery Zoé Zuniga (2013)

—— *My Cousins Fuentes*

Junior Fuentes (1970)

Enock Montes (1972)

Reycito Fuentes (1979)

Erica Fuentes (1976)

Reynaldo (Capita) Fuentes (197

Waleska Fuentes (1979)

Vanessa Alvarenga (1981)

Gabriela Montes (1982)

Karen Fuentes (1982)

Fabiola Montes (1983)

Miguel Alvarenga (1985)

Kevin Fuentes (1987)

Willie Serrano (1990)

Marcela Serrano (1992)

The End

Epilogue

In this book, the stories are independently presented, without a common thread that ties them together, which can leave the reader without a clear conclusion. This structure reflects the disconnect between my family's personal stories, as well as the lack of closure in our lives due to loss and separation. Like the memories of someone with Alzheimer's, these stories sometimes stand on their own, fragmented and without a complete picture.

While I originally chose to leave the stories unbound, as if they could stand on their own, I now see that together they fail to fully express the pain and complexity of our family. This incompleteness is a metaphor for the emptiness of losing loved ones and facing the difficulty of remembering and reconstructing our stories. My attempt to capture these experiences on paper has been a challenge, as art sometimes cannot be easily explained. However, upon reflection, I see that these stories, despite their apparent disconnect, are a true reflection of a deeper pain in our family, a pain that only those who share our bond will fully understand. In the process, I hope that you, as a reader, will find some inspiration to become curious about your own family history and the stories that make up all those experiences lived and destined to occur. I want you to find yourself here, reading these stories that in so many ways define who we are and who we are not. May this journey through our narratives motivate you to explore your own legacy, to discover the connections and disconnections that shape your identity and that of your family.

Oscar Fuentes

Other Works by Oscar Fuentes

Beautiful Women Will Never Know (2013)
4 Nights With Betsy (2014)
Vagabond: Selected Poems, Short Stories, and Plays (2015)
Welcome Home: Poems inspired by 1Hotel South Beach (2019)
Body Furnace (2021)
For the Love of Leotards (2022)
The Cock Fight (2022)
Oscar The Clown (2022)
Honey & Sting: Short Stories and Poems (2023)

About the Author

© Marcello Cassano

Born in Manhattan, New York, to immigrant parents from Honduras, Oscar Fuentes is a multidisciplinary artist based in Miami, who has been sharing his talents and love of the arts for more than 30 years. Known by his moniker, The Biscayne Poet, Oscar has dedicated more than three decades to sharing his talents and passion for the arts. He is the author of eight books of poetry and prose, including *Beautiful Women Will Never Know* (2013), *4 Nights With Betsy* (2014), *Vagabond: Selected Poems, Short Stories, and Plays* (2015), *Welcome Home: Poems inspired by 1Hotel South Beach* (2019), *For the Love of Leotards* (2022) and *Honey & Sting: Short Stories and Poems* (2023). Oscar has also been featured in illustrated zine publications such as, *Body Furnace* (2021), *The Cock Fight* (2022), and *Oscar The Clown* (2022).

Oscar was also recognized by Mayor Daniella Levine Cava with the inaugural Miami-Dade Mayoral Poetry Commendation in recognition of outstanding contributions to the county's literary art community. He is represented by Indie Earth Publishing and uses typewriter tape for a mustache.

Connect with Oscar on Social: @thebiscaynepoet

www.thebiscaynepoet.com

About the Publisher

Indie Earth Publishing is an independent, author-first co-publishing company based in Miami, FL, dedicated to giving authors and writers the creative freedom they deserve. Indie Earth combines the freedom of self-publishing with the support and backing of traditional publishing for poetry, fiction, and short story collections by providing a plethora of services meant to aid them in the book publishing experience. With Indie Earth Publishing, you are more than just another author, you are part of the Indie Earth creative family, making a difference one book at a time.

www.indieearthbooks.com

Instagram: @indieearthbooks

For inquiries, please email:
indieearthbooks@gmail.com

9 798989 555185